FREIGHT TRAINS

by Darlene R. Stille

Content Adviser: Professor Sherry L. Field,
Department of Social Science Education, College of Education,
The University of Georgia
Reading Adviser: Dr. Linda D. Labbo,
Department of Reading Education, College of Education,
The University of Georgia

Compass Point Books

Minneapolis, Minnesota

Compass Point Books
3722 West 50th Street, #115
Minneapolis, MN 55410

Visit Compass Point Books on the Internet at *www.compasspointbooks.com* or e-mail your request to *custserv@compasspointbooks.com*

Editors: E. Russell Primm and Emily J. Dolbear
Photo Researcher: Svetlana Zhurkina
Photo Selector: Melissa Voda
Designer: Melissa Voda

Library of Congress Cataloging-in-Publication Data
Stille, Darlene R.
    Freight trains / by Darlene R. Stille.
        p. cm. — (Transportation)
    1. Railroads—Juvenile literature. [1. Railroads—Trains.] I. Title.
TF148 .S838 2001
625.1—dc21   2001001433

Here Comes a Train!

Here we are at a railroad crossing! Bells are clang-ing, red lights are flashing. A gate comes down. Stop! A train is coming. Hear the train whistle. See the bright lights on the train's engine. It thunders down the track.

Kinds of Locomotives

The first locomotives were called steam engines. They burned wood or coal to make steam for power. They gave off black smoke that made the air dirty.

Today locomotives burn diesel fuel made from oil. Diesel locomotives can be hooked together. Then they can pull long freight trains.

This Is a Freight Train

This train is a freight train. Passenger trains carry people. Freight trains carry everything from food to coal to new cars. The cargo that a freight train carries is called freight.

This train is a long train. It has many railroad cars hooked together. Some freight trains have as many as 200 cars.

Here Comes a Boxcar!

A boxcar has four sides. It has a floor on the bottom and a roof on top. It looks like a box on wheels.

A boxcar keeps freight clean and dry. Radios and television sets are carried in boxcars. Food is carried in boxcars too.

A Special Boxcar

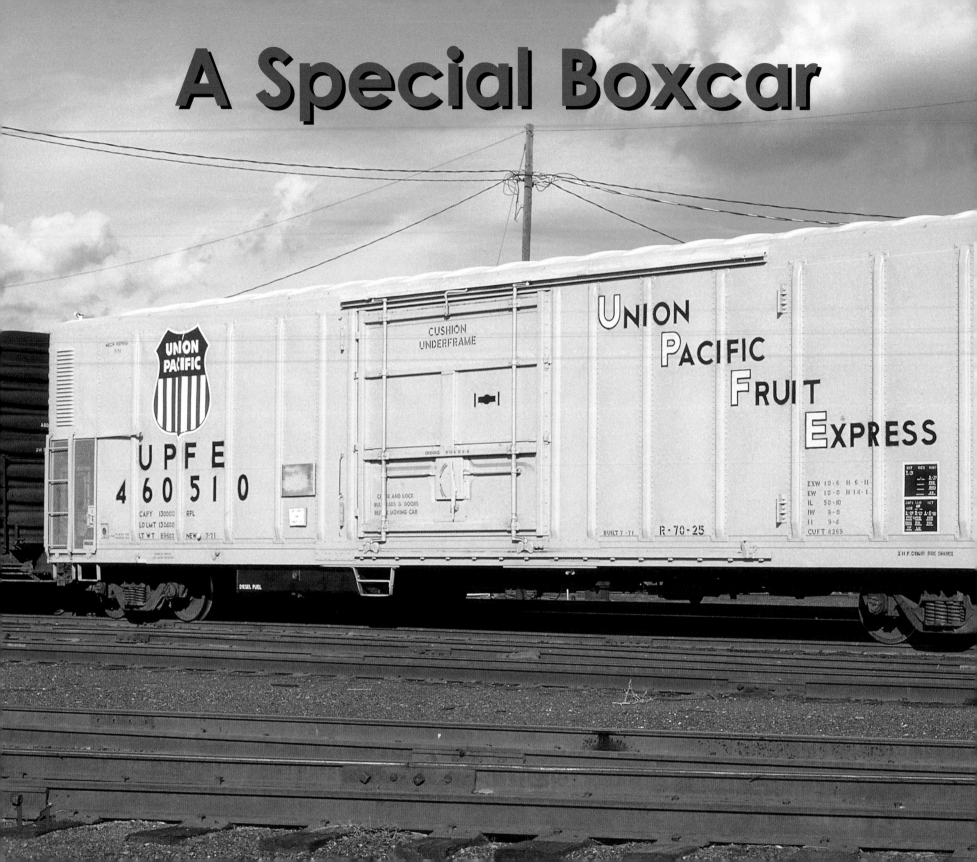

Some boxcars are made to carry food. Some even have the word "refrigerator" printed on the side. Refrigerator boxcars are as cold inside as your refrigerator at home.

Refrigerator cars carry food that must be kept cold. They carry meat, fruit, and frozen foods.

Here Comes a Flatcar!

flatcar

A flatcar looks like a big tabletop on wheels. It has no roof. It does not even have sides.

Cranes load lumber and steel onto flatcars. Flatcars can also carry huge machines. Special flatcars are made to carry cars, boats, trucks, and even buses.

Here Comes a Tank Car!

UTLX 12403

CAPY 14732 GAL US
55 767 LITERS

SPRG D-3
36" WHLS
SF 70 CC COUPLERS

CHROMIUM TRIOXIDE ANHYDROUS

1463
5.1

A tank car looks like a big, round tank lying on its side. A tank car carries liquids or gases.

Tank cars carry milk, gasoline, or oil, for example. Some tank cars carry dangerous chemicals.

The Train Track

rails

ties

spikes

Train Wheels

Locomotives and train cars have wheels made of metal. When the wheels roll, the train moves.

The wheels also hold the train on the track. The wheels are shaped to fit over the rails. This shape keeps the train from slip-ping off the track.

There Goes the Train!

Index

About the Author

Darlene R. Stille is a science editor and writer. She has lived in Chicago, Illinois, all her life. When she was in high school, she fell in love with science. While attending the University of Illinois, she discovered that she also enjoyed writing. Today she feels fortunate to have a career that allows her to pursue both her interests. Darlene R. Stille has written more than thirty books for young people.

Copyright ©2000 by Nord-Süd Verlag AG, Gossau Zürich, Switzerland
First published in Switzerland under the title *Die Zwergen Mütze*
English translation copyright ©2000 by North-South Books Inc.

First published in the United States, Great Britain, Canada,
Australia, and New Zealand in 2000 by North-South Books,
an imprint of Nord-Süd Verlag AG, Gossau Zürich, Switzerland.

Distributed in the United States by North-South Books Inc., New York.

Library of Congress Cataloging-in-Publication Data is available.
A CIP catalogue record for this book is available from The British Library.
ISBN 0-7358-1254-3 (trade binding) 10 9 8 7 6 5 4 3 2 1
ISBN 0-7358-1255-1 (library binding) 10 9 8 7 6 5 4 3 2 1
Printed in Italy

For more information about our books, and the authors and artists
who create them, visit our web site: www.northsouth.com

A Michael Neugebauer Book

North-South Books / New York / London

THE ELF'S HAT

Adapted by Brigitte Weninger

Illustrated by John A. Rowe

Translated by J. Alison James

One fine day an elf went for a walk.
As he trundled through the woods,
a low-hanging branch brushed his
hat off his head.

The elf never noticed,
and the hat lay where it fell.

A frog hopped by.
He saw the empty hat.
"Croak, croak!
A lovely place to sleep!" he said.
"A wonderful house for me alone!"
And he hopped inside his
warm new home.

Not long after, a mouse ran by.
She saw the lumpy hat and squeaked.
"A home-in-a-hat? Imagine that!
Squeak, squeak! Hello in there.
Do you have some room to spare?"
The frog looked out of the hat.
"Yes!" he said. "Come in, come in!"

Next a hare came hopping past.
He saw the lumpy hat,
twitched his nose, and said,
"A home-in-a-hat? Imagine that!
Twitch, twitch! Hello in there.
Do you have some room to spare?"
The frog and mouse looked out
of the hat.
"Yes, yes!" they said. "Come in, come in!"

Then a hedgehog ambled by.
He saw the lumpy hat and sniffed.
"A home-in-a-hat? Imagine that!
Sniff, sniff! Hello in there.
Do you have some room to spare?"
The frog
and mouse
and hare
looked out of the hat.
"Yes, yes, yes!" they said.
"Come in, come in!"

A crow then landed on the ground.
She saw the lumpy hat and cawed.
"A home-in-a-hat? Imagine that!
Caw, caw! Hello in there.
Do you have some room to spare?"
The frog
and mouse
and hare
and hedgehog looked out of the hat.
"Yes, yes, yes, yes!" they said.
"Come in, come in!"

Right after that, a fox crept up.
He saw the lumpy hat and yipped.
"A home-in-a-hat? Imagine that!
Yip, yip! Hello in there.
Do you have some room to spare?"
The frog
and mouse
and hare
and hedgehog
and crow looked out of the hat.
"Yes, yes, yes, yes, yes!" they said.
"Come in, come in!"

Then a boar ran by.
She saw the lumpy hat and grunted.
"A home-in-a-hat? Imagine that!
Grunt, grunt! Hello in there.
Do you have some room to spare?"
The frog
and mouse
and hare
and hedgehog
and crow
and fox looked out of the hat.
"Yes, yes, yes, yes, yes, yes!" they said.
"Come in, come in!"

All of a sudden a wolf dashed by.
He saw the lumpy hat and howled.
"A home-in-a-hat? Imagine that!
Wooo, wooo! Hello in there.
Do you have some room to spare?"
The frog
and mouse
and hare
and hedgehog
and crow
and fox
and boar looked out of the hat.
"Yes, yes, yes, yes, yes, yes, yes!" they said.
"Come in, come in!"

Then a bear lumbered through the woods.
He saw the lumpy hat and growled.
"A home-in-a-hat? Imagine that!
Grrr, grrr! Hello in there.
Do you have some room to spare?"
The frog
and mouse
and hare
and hedgehog
and crow
and fox
and boar
and wolf looked out of the hat.
"Yes, yes, yes, yes, yes, yes, yes, yes!"
they said. "Come in, come in!"

It was getting crowded
in the elf's red hat.
Very crowded!

Then up hopped a teeny-weeny flea.
She nibbled a door for herself in the hat,
then crawled inside and said,
"I'm just a teeny-weeny flea.
Surely you have room for me."

"NOOOOOO!"
The elf's hat wiggled
and jiggled . . .

. . . and out popped
the bear
and wolf

and boar
and fox
and hedgehog
and hare

and mouse
and frog,

and as fast
as they could
they ran off
through the woods!

So the flea settled in,
as happy as could be.

Around about then, the elf came back
for his missing hat.
"There you are!" he said, brushing it off
fondly. He clapped it onto his head and
kept on going, to see what he could see—
and all the way there
and all the way back
in her home-in-a-hat
went the teeny-weeny flea.
Why, just imagine that!